TO:

FROM:

DATE:

For my sons
–VALERIE ACKLEY

To my children; may you embrace the message of this book.
And to Rosalie who taught me it was okay to believe.
–LORI NAWYN

AUTHOR'S NOTE: Look closely and you will find a rabbit on each page of this story.
The rabbit represents what you want most of all. Once you know what you want, it becomes
your "rabbit." Cheerful, positive thoughts help you catch your rabbit, but sad, miserable
thoughts make it hop away. To learn more about how to attract your rabbit, go to
www.Jackrabbitfactor.com.

ISBN: 978-0-9816749-1-9
Library of Congress Control Number: 2011945129

Text copyright © 2009 by Valerie Ackley
Illustration copyright © 2009 by Lori Nawyn

All rights reserved. Published by ThoughtsAlive Books

Printed and bound in the United States of America
12 13 14 15 10 9 8 7 6 5 4 3 2 1

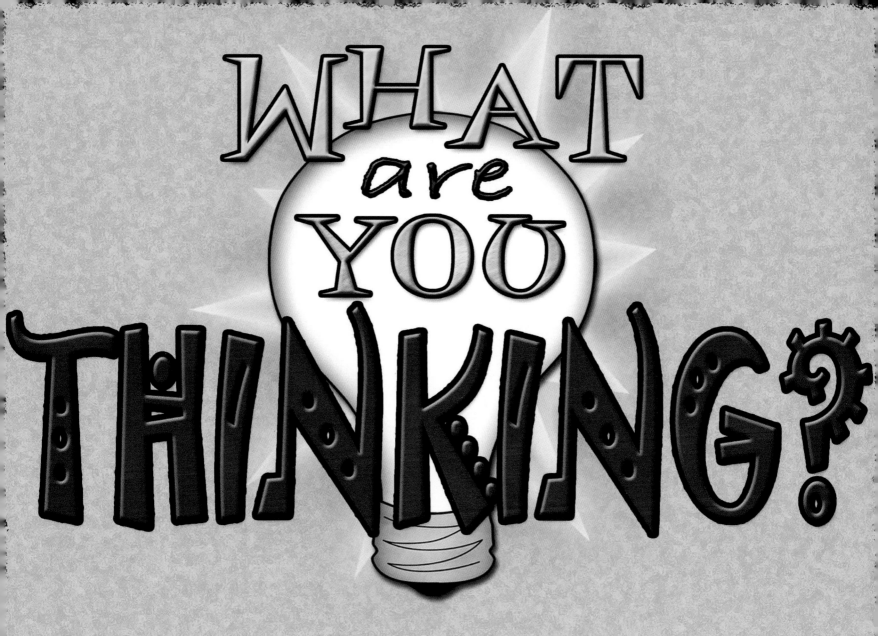

WHAT are YOU THINKING?

written by
VALERIE ACKLEY

illustrated by
LORI NAWYN

Valerie Ackley

THOUGHTSALIVE BOOKS

Did you ever really really REALLY want SOMEthiNG?

You **DREAMED, PLANNED** and **WORKED** until you finally got it!

Wish List!

New Friend

Math Champ

5k Race

New Skill

Bike

DID YOU *know* it *wasn't* just luck?

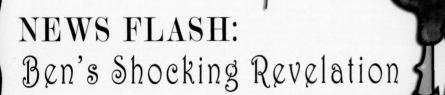

STINKY FOOT POWDER DEVELOPED! MOTHERS ALL OVER THE WORLD SAY, "THANK YOU!" and CELEBRATE WITH DAY OF REJOICING.
TRIPLE STRENGTH
stink B gone
2 KOOL SHUEZ
2 KOOL SHUEZ
Graham's idea rings a bell!
anything ever created or achieved first began as a THOUGHT!
hi mom
USA
chickens crack up over new invention
Wright stuff
NEW GAME hits home
Thought followed by ACTION has made our world a better place.

A MAGNIFYING GLASS CAN **FOCUS** THE SUN'S ENERGY TO HAVE GREAT POWER!

WHEN YOUR THOUGHTS ARE

They pull towards you ALL you need

FOCUSED THEY ALSO HAVE POWER

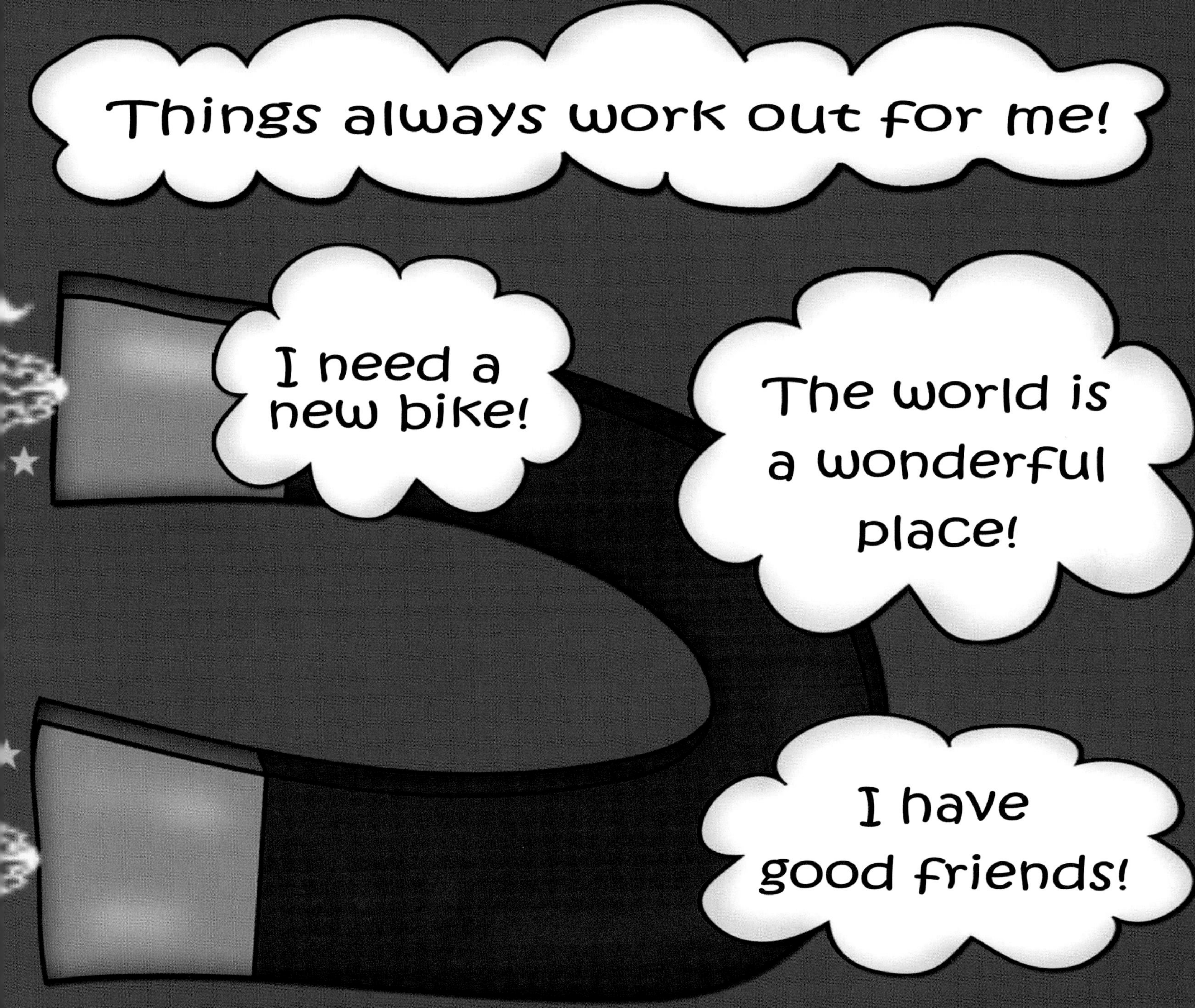

to achieve your heart's desire!

Just as a bug is

drawn to light...

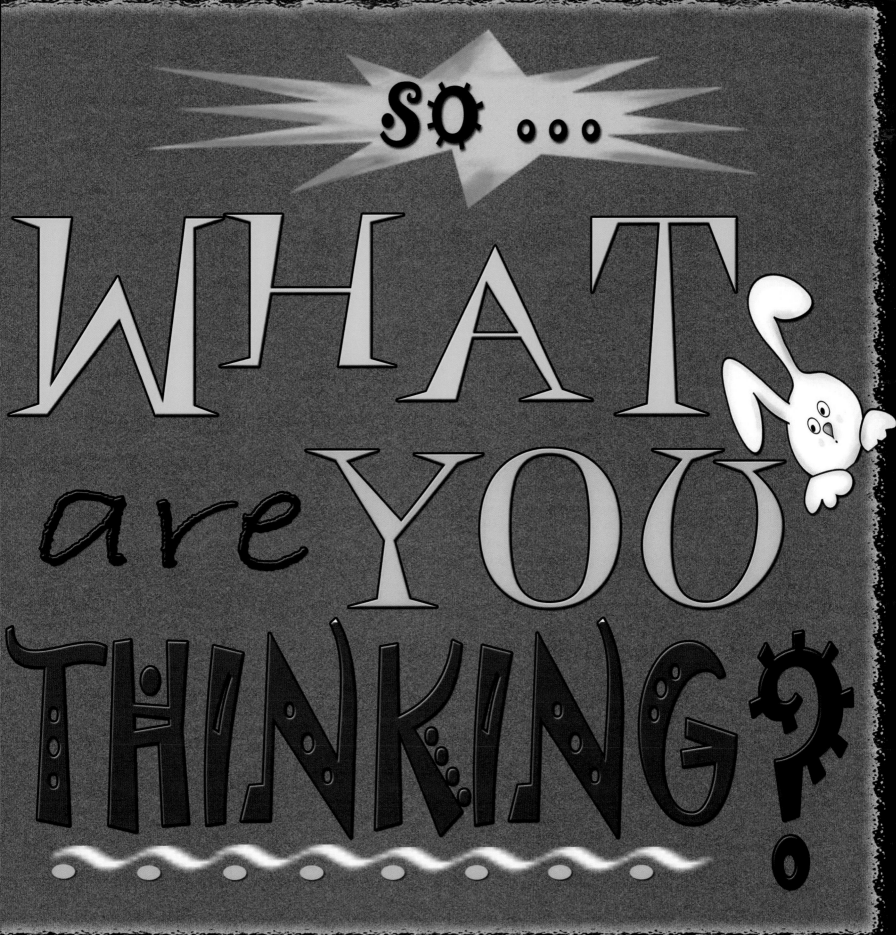

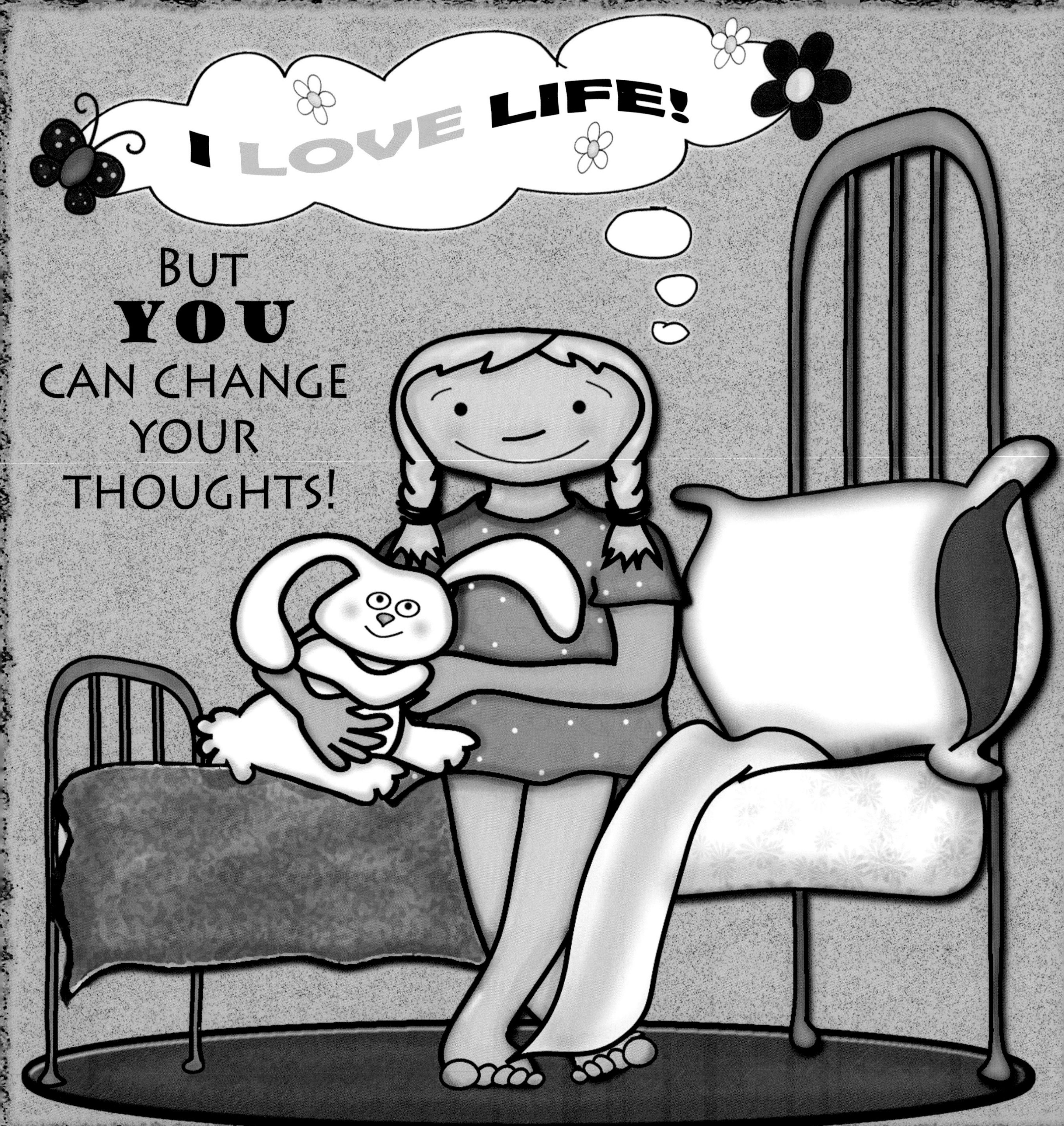
I LOVE LIFE!
BUT
YOU
CAN CHANGE
YOUR
THOUGHTS!

Granny knows that just as you can **CHOOSE** what you listen

Always tune your thoughts

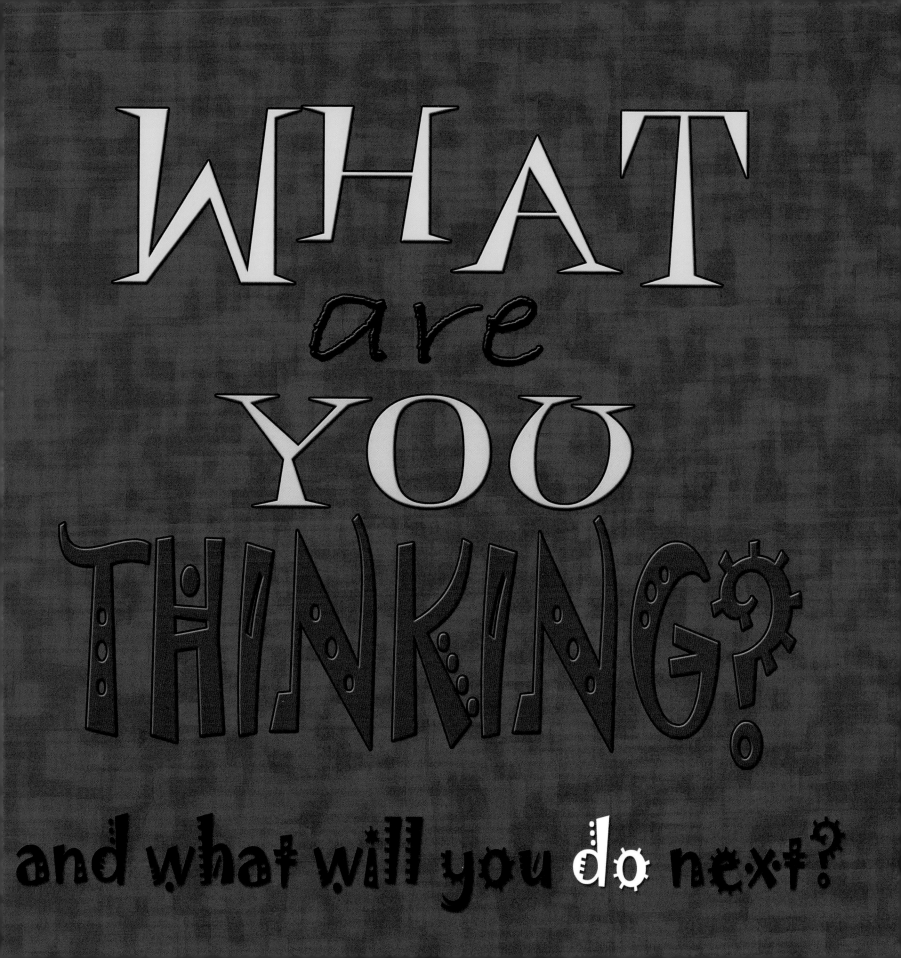